World Premier Hotel Design

Volume

2

SUPER SUITE INTERIOR

Supervision:

Noboru KAWAZOE

Photography & Text:

Hiro KISHIKAWA

KAWADE SHOBO SHINSHA

Introduction

by Noboru Kawazoe

Architectural Critic

This volume takes a look at top-class suites—Presidential Suites and Royal Suites—at various famous hotels around the world. The first part of the book introduces luxuriously appointed "super suites," while the second portion looks at famous "celebrity suites" that have been named after the famous people who stayed in them. Through the simple explanations and description captions in this book, we hope the stories told here will leave a deep impression in the reader's imagination.

One of the charms of staying in a hotel is that anyone, once they've paid for their room, can feel like royalty. To help foster these feelings, hotels are constantly striving for more impressive and more elegant interiors. The public spaces in a hotel—the banquet rooms and reception halls—were originally provided to match the facilities one would find in a royal palace or an aristrocratic estate, as hotels were originally created to serve royalty and the aristocracy.

While people today, especially Japanese people, tend to think of fashion as being a set of popular trends embraced by the general public, in olden times fashions tended to start among the upper classes and be passed down and copied by the masses. The roots of present-day European urban culture are tied to the absolute monarchies of history—the Bourbon dynasty in France, the Tudors in England, the Hapsburgs in Austrian and the Romanoffs in Russia. The class of feudal lords, natural adversaries of the royalty, were subtly coopted as they were invited to garden parties, dances, and concerts in the royal palaces, where they had the opportunity to exercise the manners and etiquette appropriate to their social position. King Louis XIV single-handedly influenced his country's taste in design with his creation of the Royal Academy, and he also purchased the Gobelins tapestry manufactory, where royal artisans from various parts of the country were gathered together to create furnishings and tableware for the royal palace. Even today you can find shops selling items from Royal Copenhagen, which was established in a similar manner. The king would also have his own set of royal architects, interior designers, fashion designers, cooks and hairdressers, and they would change when a new king was crowned. And just as Louis XIV style was baroque and Louis XV style was rococo, design styles would change, and the aristocracy and eventually the masses would follow those shifts in fashion. This was the beginning of European fashion trends.

The first real urban hotels, owned by companies independent of the royal court, were the Grand Hotel in Paris, built in 1862, the Hotel de Louvre (planned by Napoleon III), built in 1855, and the Kaiser Hotel in Berlin, built in 1874. Hotels naturally carried on certain traditions based on their historical connections with the royal palaces. This history is the basis for the "King's Room" or the "Presidential Suite" in many hotels. And while other Royal Suites or Presidential Suites may not have the same sort of history, somewhow there is still the spirit of royalty and nobility in these lavishly appointed rooms.

But what is that "spirit"? Various places seem to have their own distinctive atmosphere, and Japanese people often think about their "self" as including a portion of their immediate environment as well as their own person (what's called a "second self"). But perhaps Japanese, compared to Westerners, have a weaker attachment to material possessions, and a sense that the fleeting mood is just as important. Westerners have a greater tendency to preserve the houses or rooms where famous people have lived, even if they are hotel rooms. At any rate, hotels are special places where one can relax completely, or alternatively they're places where one can find a new "second self" and indulge in self-discovery in a fresh environment.

Contents

SUPER SUITES IN ASIA

Chapter 2 CELEBRITY SUPER SUITES 136

World Premier Hotel Design: Volume 2
SUPER SUITE INTERIOR

Photography & Text:
Hiro Kishikawa

Supervision:
Noboru Kawazoe

Translation:
Kenichi Sakamoto
Bjorn Katz

Art Direction:
Manami Mizuhashi

Editor:
Hiroaki Ishii

KAWADE SHOBO SHINSHA, Publishers
2-32-2, Sendagaya, Shibuya-Ku, Tokyo 151-0051, Japan

Copyright © Kawade Shobo Shinsha, Publishers 2006
Photo & Text copyright © Hiro Kishikawa 2006

Printed in China
ISBN4-309-80002-5

Right page:
The signature of selebrities in the "Golden Book."
Ritz Paris, France.

Chapter 1

WORLD VIP SUPER SUITES

The dining room of the Presidential Suite in the famous The Waldorf Towers, New York.

Photo and signature of the Duke of Kent in the "Golden Book" of the Beau Rivage Palace, Ouchy-Lausanne, Switzerland.

When the Simplon Tunnel opened in 1906 it cut by half the travel time to hotels in Italy and southern France. A railroad PR poster.
Opposite page: **The "Morning Room" of Hartwell House was used as a drawing room when it was an aristocratic mansion. It was designed by the architect Henry Keene in 1760–1763, with Rococo-style walls and ceiling. Images of a dragon, hawk, lion and dragon can be found in the four corners of the ceiling, representing the four elements of fire, wind, earth and water**

Famous hotels around the world will offer a "Presidential Suite" or a "Royal Suite" for the use of VIP guests. Some of these suites are larger than 1000 square meters, and some provide special security measures. In London the famous hotel Claridge's has a Royal Suite that's used by the British royal family so often during horse-racing season that it has been given the nickname "Buckingham Palace Annex." During a two-week period when US President Reagan stayed in the Presidential Suite in New York's landmark The Waldorf Towers, the floors above and below his suite were kept empty, and the ceilings, floors and walls were carefully checked for listening devices. It is said that for security reasons, Reagan slept in an adjoining bedroom rather than the master bedroom.

A top-class Presidential Suite may include a private lobby, a drawing room with attached toilet, a dining/meeting room, a library/study, a main bedroom with attached bath, a second bedroom with attached bath, guest bedrooms and other facilities.

The origin of these suites owes a great deal to the lifestyles of the 19th-century British Empire, when Britain ruled the Seven Seas after the Industrial Revolution. The British royalty and aristocracy of that time would travel on vacation with their wives, children, butlers, maids and other servants, and occupy hotel suites for as long as a month at a time, during which time many important meetings took place in the drawing rooms or dining rooms of the hotel suite, while the wives were enjoying afternoon tea. Hotels found it to be in their business interest to cater to the tastes of the upper classes of the British Empire, then the dominant power in the world, by providing these enormous suites along with appropriate interiors and service.

These suites, miniaturized versions of the mansions of the British aristocracy, have continued to be popular to this day. We'll start this chapter by looking at plans for Hartwell House, a converted aristocratic manor house in England, and then look at some "super suites" catering to executives and VIPs in hotels in Europe, America and Asia.

The Bourbon Room

Hartwell House
Oxford Road Aylesbury,
Buckinghamshire, HP17 8NL, England, UK
Tel: (44-1296) 747444 Fax: (44-1296) 747450
http://www.hartwell-house.com

Construction date: 1600s
Additional construction date: 1755
Architect/Designer: James Gibbs, Henry Keene, James Wyatt, Richard Wood
Opening date: 1989
Architect: Eric Throssell
Interior Design Supervision: Janey Compton
Number of rooms: 34 rooms including 13 suites
Contact the hotel directly

This aristocratic mansion hotel stands in the quiet, hilly Aylesbury area of Buckinghamshire. The name comes from the Hartwell family, which received the land on which the the mansion was built in the late 12th century from King John (son of Henry II). In the 17th century it passed into possession of the Hampden and Lee families (from which the American Civil War general Robert E. Lee was descended), and it was owned by them until 1938. The present Hartwell House was built by the Hampden family, with additional construction work in 1755. In 1989 it was converted to a hotel, and the 18th-century interiors were restored in the 33 guest rooms. Guests can also enjoy the splendid original design of four salons, where the original English baroque and rococo styles from the mid-18th century have been beautifully restored.

The back of the main building was designed in Georgian period style.

The "Bourbon Room" commemorates the stay of Louis XVIII, of the Bourbon family. The room is decorated in Georgian period neo-classical style, with Louis XV style sofas and Louis XVI style armchairs. The room features a dressing area, furnished with long drapes, in the bay window area.

Hartwell House from around 1730. The Great Hall and Morning Room were added later.

Right page: **The "Great Hall," designed by architect James Gibbs in English Baroque style in 1739–1740. The decorative plasterwork on the ceiling is the work of two Italian artisans, Giovanni Bagutti and Giuseppe Artari. This space was used for banquets by General Lee.**

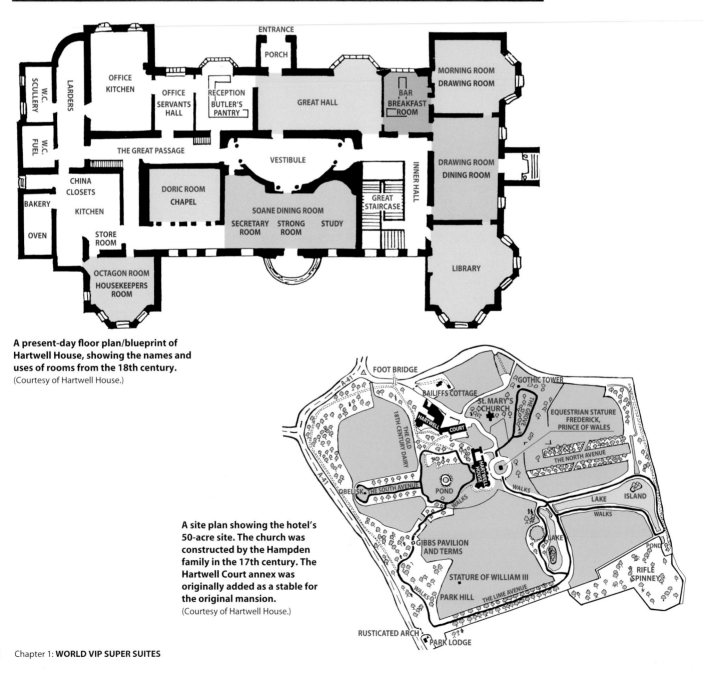

A present-day floor plan/blueprint of Hartwell House, showing the names and uses of rooms from the 18th century.
(Courtesy of Hartwell House.)

A site plan showing the hotel's 50-acre site. The church was constructed by the Hampden family in the 17th century. The Hartwell Court annex was originally added as a stable for the original mansion.
(Courtesy of Hartwell House.)

The Neo-classical style vestibule with bay window was designed by architect James Wyatt in 1780. This space is now the "Private Lobby" of the Presidential Suite.

The historical library where the exiled King Louis XVIII signed constitutional documents confirming his ascension to the throne. The gilt-edged bookshelf is a valuable antique from the late Georgian period.

The Kings Room

Hartwell House
Oxford Road Aylesbury,
Buckinghamshire, HP17 8NL, England, UK
Tel: (44-1296) 747444   Fax: (44-1296) 747450
http://www.hartwell-house.com

An armchair with unusual carvings.

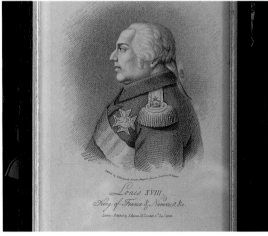

Portraits of French King Louis XVIII (Louis Xavier Stanislas; 1755–1824; reigned 1814–1815) hang on either side of the fireplace. He is better known as the younger brother of Louis XVI.

The King's Room (Number 15) was built in commemoration of the stay of King Louis XVIII while he was in exile. Along with King Louis and his queen, hundreds of distinguished exiled aristocrats spent time here. Remembering his days of exile here once he had returned to France, he is said to have commented that he wanted to return to Hartwell House.

Presidential Suite

The Balmoral
1 Princes Street, Edinburgh EH2 2EQ, Scotland, U,K,
Tel: (44-131) 556-2414   Fax: (44-131) 557-8740
http://www.lhw.com/balmoral

Opening date: November 15, 1902
Architect: Beattie & Scott
Renovation date: 1988–1991
Food & beverage facilities: 4
Guest rooms: 188 (including 20 suites)
Contact: The Leading Hotels of the World

This early station hotel was built by the North British Railway company on Princes Street in Edinburgh. According to the company, at the time of its opening it had 300 guest rooms, 53 baths and 70 toilets. In 1988, after three years of renovation work, the hotel reopened with a more modern interior design, newly renovated restaurants, lounges and bars, and a reduced number of guest rooms. The lobby and the ballroom were restored to their original design. In 1997 it was bought by the Rocco Forte Hotels. The guest rooms all feature high celings, and the Presidential Suite is lavishly appointed with a drawing room, bedroom, wardrobe room and bath.

The facade of the Balmoral. The clock tower is visible from all over town; it is part of the face of Edinburgh.

The large fireplace in the drawing room of the Presidential Suite.

Toilet, bidet and shower stall in the bathroom.

The spacious bathroom features
a claw-foot bathtub.

French Flag Suite

Hotel de Crillon
10, Place de la Concorde-75008 Paris, France
Tel: (33-1) 44-71 -15-00 Fax: (33-1) 44-71-15-02
http://www.concordehotels.com

Construction date: 1785
Architect: Ange-Jacques Gabriel
Opening date: 1909
Renovation Architect: Destailleurs
Food & beverage facilities: 4
Guest rooms: 160, 51 suites
Contact: Concorde Hotels

The Hotel de Crillon, completed in 1785, was designed by the architect Jacques-Ange Gabriel, who was commissioned by King Louis XV. The young Marie Antoinette, slipping away from her music lessons in the nearby Louvre, came to the private dining room here for breaks. (The former dining room, on the second floor, is now the "Salon Marie Antoinette.") It was here on the Place de la Concorde where she married King Louis XVI and it was also here where she met her final fate and was executed.

The top-class French Flag Suite look out over the Place de la Concorde from the third story. The interiors are decorated in the colors of the flag: blue (Suite Pajotterie), white (Suite Pigarniere) and red (Suite Marqueterie), and the achievements of the Bourbon Dynasty are displayed in the lovely Louis XV and Louis XVI style interiors.

Two historic buildings on the Place de la Concorde; to the right is the French Naval Ministry, and to the left the Hotel de Crillon.

The drawing room of the Suite Pajotterie, with Louis XVI style furniture and Louis XV style gilt decorative details on the walls and ceiling.

A Louis XVI style chair in the Suite Pajotterie. The chest of drawers is a 19th-century antique, a Louis XV style bombe commode, so called because of its bulbous shape.

The bedroom of the Suite Marqueterie is decorated in red fabric.

The bathroom of the Suite Pigarniere, furnished with a double sink, bathtub and shower stall. Bath amenities are by Annick Goutal.

A view of Place de la Concorde from the Suite Pajotterie. The domed structure is where Napoleon's tomb is located, part of the Invalides hospital.

Right page: A sitting area in the corner of the drawing room of the Suite Pigarniere. The chairs are reproductions of Louis XVI style bergere a oreilles pieces from the 18th century.

The drawing room of the Suite Marqueterie is decorated in red fabrics; the wall and ceiling cornice decorations are Louis XV style. Behind the right-hand door is the suite's private lobby.

Presidential Suite

Kempinski Hotel Taschenbergpalais Dresden
Taschenberg 3, 01067 Dresden, Germany
Tel: (49-351) 49-12-0   Fax: (49-351) 49-12-812
http://www.lhw.com/kempdres

Reconstruction date: 1995
Developer: Firm Advanta, Frankfurt
Interior design: AB Living Designs, Sweden
Food & beverage facilities: 6
Guest rooms: 182, 32 suites
Contact: The Leading Hotels of the World

The hotel occupies a historic building that was originally built in the 18th century by Saxon King August I for use as the reception hall for the royal palace. Damaged by bombing during World War II, it was beautifully restored at the time of German reunification. While the exterior is a faithful reproduction of its original appearance, the interior is much more modern in design. The 340-square-meter Presidential Suite contains seven rooms-four bedrooms, two drawing rooms and a private lobby-all decorated in different colored fabrics.

The hotel entrance.

A drawing room (Number 245), with desk, sitting area and dining area. The right-hand door leads to a green-themed bedroom.

The main bedroom (Number 239), decorated in red fabric.

An anteroom (Number 243) adjoining the suite's private lobby.

A bedroom (Number 240) decorated in yellow fabric.

The suite's fourth bedroom (Number 244), decorated in green.
There is a sitting area in the far right-hand corner.

The private lobby, located near the middle of the suite.

Presidential Suite

Grand Hotel National
Haldenstrasse 4, CH-6000 Luzern, Switzerland
Tel: (41-41) 419 0909   Fax: (41-41) 419 0910
http://www.worldhotelsgroup.com

Opening date: 1870
Architect: Maximilian-Alphons Pfyffer
Renovation date: 1979
Food & beverage facilities: 4
Guest rooms: 80, 8 suites, 40 residential apartments
Contact: Worldhotel

Hotel owner Maximilian-Alphons Pfyffer, who was also the architect, hired the team of Cesar Ritz (later known as the "hotel king") and noted chef August Escoffier to run the Grand Hotel National, and together they revolutionized the hotel world. More than a century later, in 1979, the hotel was renovated by its new owner, and at that time the Presidential Suite and the residential apartments were added. The residential apartments, billed as "contemporary residences in the middle of a famous hotel," were a bold new experiment in the hotel world at the time.

The Hotel National was built during lakefront development in the 1860s. The left half of the building was added in the 1900s.

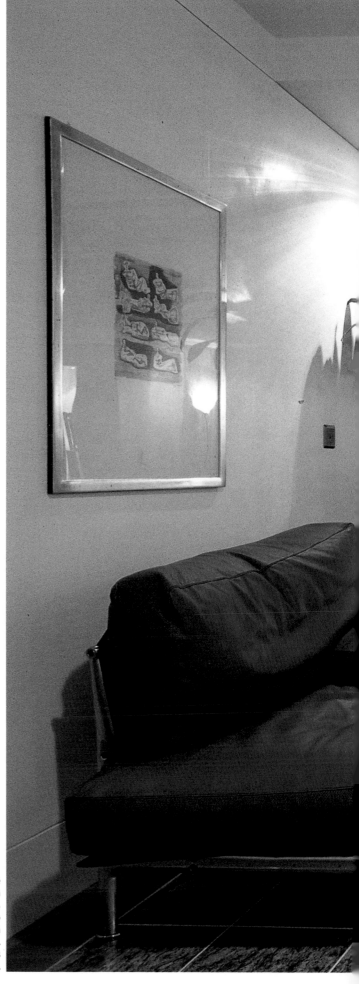

A view of the drawing room from the private lobby, flanked by two reddish-brown columns. The frosted glass door is automatic.

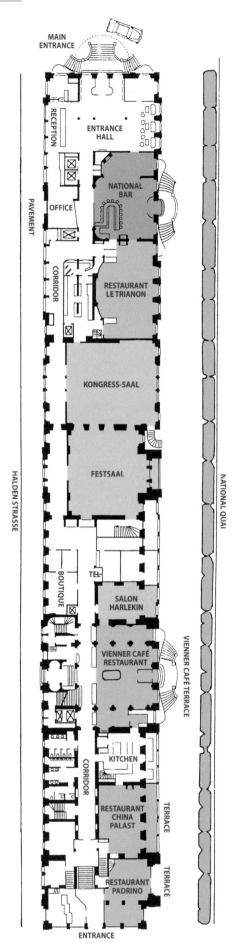

MAIN ENTRANCE

RECEPTION

ENTRANCE HALL

PAVEMENT

OFFICE

NATIONAL BAR

CORRIDOR

RESTAURANT LE TRIANON

HALDEN STRASSE

KONGRESS-SAAL

NATIONAL QUAI

FESTSAAL

BOUTIQUE

TEL

SALON HARLEKIN

VIENNER CAFÉ TERRACE

VIENNER CAFÉ RESTAURANT

CORRIDOR

KITCHEN

TERRACE

RESTAURANT CHINA PALAST

TERRACE

RESTAURANT PADRINO

ENTRANCE

Floor plan of the ground floor. The Presidential Suite is located on the fifth floor of the Entrance Hall. (Courtesy of Grand Hotel National.)

A contemporary armchair and antique inlaid "cabinet on stand" at the entrance to the drawing room. The antique furnishings probably date back to 1890s Italy.
Right page: The ultra-modern kitchen is done in a blue color scheme.

The main bedroom, one of three bedrooms in the suite.

A dolphin-themed mosaic adorns the bottom of the jacuzzi.

Located off the stairway between the fifth and sixth floors is an eight-seat private theater.
Right page: **A fresco painting in the jacuzzi room is fashioned after the view from a mansion atop a hill in Pompeii.**

A gym next to the jacuzzi room; there is also a sauna room.

Villa La Cupola

The Westin Excelsior, Rome
Via Vittorio Veneto 125, Rome 00187, Italy
Tel: (39-06) 47081   Fax: (39-06) 482 6205
http://www.starwoodhotels.com

Opening date: 1906
Architect: Firm of Vogt & Otto Maliani
Villa La Cupola interior design: Michael Stelea
Food & beverage facilities: 3
Guest rooms: 321 (including 45 suites)
Contact: Starwood Hotels & Resorts

This white building located on Rome's fashionable grand boulevard Via Vittorio Venteto reached 100 years of in 2006. In December 1997 American architect Michael Stelea designed a huge suite to be created around the cupola; the 739-square-meter suite took one year to complete. The themes of the fresco paintings on the inner walls and ceiling of the cupola are a unique meeting of ancient Roman mythology and modern technology. The suite was contructed for the use of state guests and VIPs visiting Rome. A number of embassy buildings are located along the Via Vittorio Venteto, including the American Embassy next door to the hotel, so the location is convenient for visiting guests of state. Up to six adjoining bedrooms can be attached to the Villa La Cupola, with a total area of 1100 square meters, to accommodate large groups.

The seven-story hotel, seen from Via Vittorio Veneto. The hotel's cupola is the ceiling of the drawing room of the suite.

A roof garden, jacuzzi room and other facilities are located on the fifth-floor rooftop.

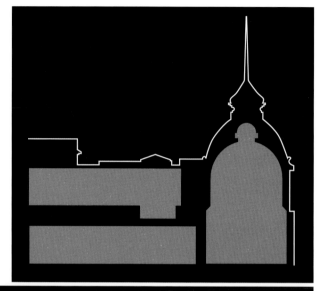

A floor plan of the hotel's fifth and sixth floors, where Villa La Cupola is located. Six bedrooms can be connected to the suite. Above right, a side view.
(Courtesy of The Westin Excelsior, Rome.)

1 • Foyer
2 • Hallway
3 • Master bedroom
4 • Luggage room
5 • Elevator
6 • Butler pantry
7 • Dining-boardroom
8 • Bedroom
9 • Cupola
10 • Study-library
11 • Terrace
11a • Terrace-sun deck
12 • Guest bedroom
13 • Private cinema
14 • Relaxation and jacuzzi area
15 • Sauna and steam bath
16 • Fitness area

Suite

Terraces

Additional guest bedrooms

6TH FLOOR

5TH FLOOR

The dining room is furnished with a Murano glass chandelier and an inlaid marble table.

Warm-looking wood grains are featured in the library's coffered ceiling, bookcases, walls and floor.

The drawing room features a floor made from two types of marble, Corinthian pillars and classic-style curtains.

Wrapping around the top of the cornice in the drawing room are frescos in Roman Empire, Renaissance, Baroque and Neo-Classical style, and on the dome ceiling are eight unusual frescos representing a meeting of ancient Roman mythology with modern technology, depicting Zeus and electronics, Atlas and television, Venus and the movies, and so on.

The master bedroom, with four-poster bed, writing desk, sitting area, makeup table and so on. Next to it is a second bedroom with a contrasting, deep-blue color scheme.

The five-story hotel building and an outdoor pool. La Suite Palmeraie is on the third floor. The poolside restaurant's name, "Les Trois Palmiers," is taken from the three palm trees beside the pool.

La Suite Palmeraie

La Mamounia
Avenue Bab Jdid, Marrakech, Morocco
Tel: (212-44) 38-86-00 Fax: (212-44) 44-49-40
http://www.lhw.com/lamamounia

Opening date: 1923
Architect: A. Marchisio & Henri Prost
Additional construction and renovation dates: 1953, 1977
Food & beverage facilities: 12
Guest rooms: 171, 57 suites, 3 villas
Contact: The Leading Hotels of the World

The hotel's main entrance, viewed from the shops near the arched gate. To the left is the entrance to the former hotel building.

Known in colonial days as the finest winter resort in the Maghreb, La Mamounia has undergone numerous renovations, and has been transformed into a casino resort hotel. Beside the pool are three VIP villas, and inside the main building are 57 suites, including nine special "theme suites" with coordinated interior designs.

The biggest of the suites, La Suite Palmeraie (Room 280), has an area of 250 square meters; the name refers to a grove of palm trees growing in a desert oasis. The suite features a long private lobby with a conversation salon at the far end, a drawing room, a master bedroom with bath, a library, a dining room, a wardrobe room, a spare bedroom with bath, and a balcony. The elegant 32-square-meter balcony offers a view of the hotel garden and the Atlas Mountains.

At the heart of the long, narrow private lobby is a small sitting area with an oval sofa.

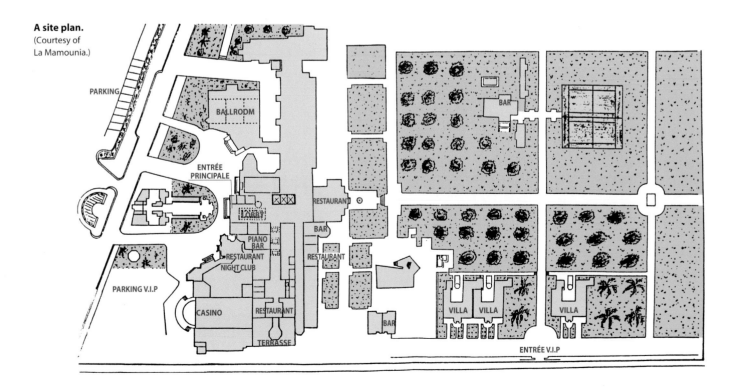

A site plan.
(Courtesy of
La Mamounia.)

PARKING

BALLRODM

ENTRÉE
PRINCIPALE

RESTAURANT

BAR

PIANO
BAR

RESTAURANT

NIGHT CLUB

RESTAURANT

PARKING V.I.P

CASINO

RESTAURANT

BAR

TERRASSE

BAR

BAR

VILLA   VILLA

VILLA

ENTRÉE V.I.P

The main bedroom of La Suite Palmeraie. The bed is called a Corona Bed, after the sun-ray pattern of the fabric on top portion of the bed. On the left is an exit leading to the private lobby, and to the right is the bathroom. The right-hand door is connected to the drawing room, with its 32-square-meter balcony.

The corona bed in the main bedroom.
On the table is a control panel with switches to
control lighting, air conditioning and so on.

The library features a Louis XV style desk.

Near the center of the main
building is a Moorish
designed waterfall, and
around it is a theme suite.

The second bedroom includes a canopy bed
and an attached bathroom.
Right page: The drawing room features trompe
l'oeil paintings on the ceiling cornice and
Louis XVI style furniture. The right-hand door
leads to the library, and that on the left leads
to the dining room and dressing room.

The second bedroom is furnished with a canopy bed and a Louis XV style sofa and table. The white cylindrical device in the left corner is a heater. On the wardrobe are red and blue ribbons, which are used as door tags. The red ribbon means "do not disturb" and the blue one means "please clean the room."

Presidential Suite

JW Marriott Ihilani   Resort & Spa at Ko Olina
92-1001 Olani Street, Ko Olina-Oahu, Hawaii 96707, USA
Tel: (1-808) 679-0079   Fax: (1-808) 679-0080
http://www.marriott.com

Opening date: December, 1993
Architect: Killingsworth, Stricker, Lindgren,
Wilson and Associates Architect Inc.
Interior design: Gasly Mebery & Associates
Food & beverage facilities: 5
Guest rooms: 387 (including 42 suites)
Contact: Marriott Hotels & Resorts

This white resort hotel, sitting on a crescent-shaped beach in one corner of the huge 2,600,000-square-meter grounds of the Ko Olina resort, has a distinctive resort feeling to it. Facilities include the Ko Olina Golf Course, designed by Ted Robinson, and the Ihilani Spa. It was originally owned by Japan Airlines, but it was purchased in 1999, six years after it opened, by Marriott Corp,.

The top-floor Presidential Suite includes a charming roof garden. In addition to room service there are also facilities to hold cocktail parties. On the night table is a control panel handling telephone, lighting, ceiling fans and air conditioning. Of course all the latest technology for voice mail and similar services is provided.

The hotel stands on a newly developed crescent-shaped beach, with 14 floors above ground and two below. The top-floor roof garden belongs to the Presidential Suite.
Right: **The white-framed roof garden of the Presidential Suite has a T-shaped plan, and is set up to provide perfect views of the sun over the horizon.**

The dining room of the
Presidential Suite is furnished
with Queen Anne chairs; the
breakfront bookcase used to
display dishes was originally
used for boks.

Carpets are spread over
the tile floor of the
Presidential Suite's
drawing room. The suite
also includes a private
lobby, a dining room
and a library.

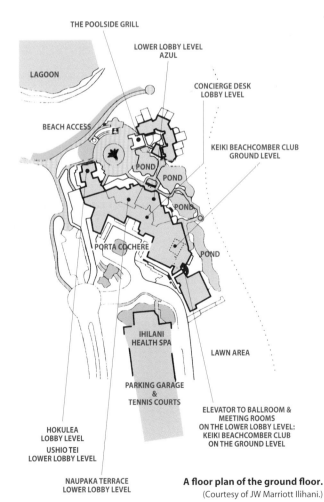

THE POOLSIDE GRILL

LOWER LOBBY LEVEL
AZUL

LAGOON

CONCIERGE DESK
LOBBY LEVEL

BEACH ACCESS

KEIKI BEACHCOMBER CLUB
GROUND LEVEL

POND

POND

POND

POND

PORTA COCHERE

IHILANI
HEALTH SPA

LAWN AREA

PARKING GARAGE
&
TENNIS COURTS

ELEVATOR TO BALLROOM &
MEETING ROOMS
ON THE LOWER LOBBY LEVEL;
KEIKI BEACHCOMBER CLUB
ON THE GROUND LEVEL

HOKULEA
LOBBY LEVEL

USHIO TEI
LOWER LOBBY LEVEL

NAUPAKA TERRACE
LOWER LOBBY LEVEL

A floor plan of the ground floor.
(Courtesy of JW Marriott Ilihani.)

A sitting area of the library/study. In the front corner is the master bedroom.

The master bedroom, with a king-size bed and a contemporary-style easy-chair and footrest.

The simply designed second bedroom includes a television cabinet built into the wall.

The spacious bathroom attached to the second bedroom includes a shower stall, bathtub and triple sink.
There's also a separate toilet and a powder room.

The Hapuna Suite includes a private
pool. Opening the sliding door
leads to a sitting space; above is the
balcony of the master bedroom.

Hapuna Suite

Hapuna Beach Prince Hotel
62-100 Kauna'oa Drive, Kohala, Coast, Hawaii 96743, USA
Tel: (1-808) 880-1111 Fax: (1-808) 880-3142
http://www.princeresorthawaii.com

Opening date: December, 1994
Architect: Wimberly, Allison, Tong & Goo
Environment design: Sasaki Environment Design Office
Food & beverage facilities: 5
Guest rooms: 351 (including 36 suites and Hapuna Suite)
Contact: Prince Hotels, Inc.

Popular with Hollywood movie stars, the hotel
provides full security measures, private check-in
service, and a private drive leading to the villa. The
three bedrooms on the second floor are set up for
movie stars to stay with their families, plus security
staff. Any requests for food are taken care of directly
by the hotel's kitchen staff.

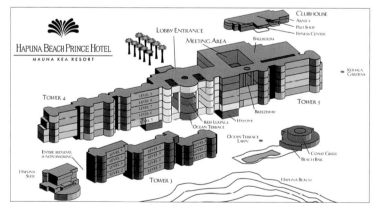

**A bird's-eye view of the hotel. The red structure on
the lower left is the Hapuna Suite.** (Courtesy of Hapuna Beach Prince Hotel.)

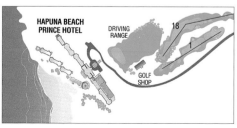

**A site plan for the hotel.
Immediately to the north
is the Mauna Kea Beach
Resort, under the same
management.**

The suite has four separate sitting areas.

A combination dining room and meeting area; this level includes a large dining area and kitchen.

The master bedroom, on the second floor;
double doors lead to a powder area on the left side.

The bathroom area of the master bedroom.

The Penthouse Suite

The Regent Beverly Wilshire
9500 WilshireBoulevard, Beverly Hills, California 90212 USA
Tel: (1-310) 275-5200   Fax: (1-310) 274-2851
http://www.regenthotels.com

Opening date: 1927
Developer: Walter G. McCarty
Architect: Walker & Eisen
Additional construction date: 1971
Renovation date: 1998
Interior design: Hirsch Bedner & Associates
Food & beverage facilities: 3
Guest rooms: 395 rooms (including 137 suites)
Contact: Four Seasons Hotels & Resorts

Famous as the setting for the film "Pretty Woman," this hotel is well suited to the gaudy film capital of Hollywood. The film was an international hit, and after its debut in 1990 the hotel became popular with honeymooners from around the world.

The hotel has a complicated history—it was originally built as the Beverly Wilshire Apartment Hotel, part of the metamorphosis of the area around the huge Beverly Auto Speedway into a high-priced residential neighborhood. In 1971 the Beverly Wing was added and the new name of the hotel was adopted. In 1989 the interior was completely reconstructed at a cost of $100 million, and the hotel took its present form, and in 1998 after additional investment the rooms in the Beverly Wing were completely renovated at a cost of $35 million.

During the first round of renovations, the top-class Penthouse Suite was built. Consisting of a sitting area, dining room, video room, three bedrooms and four baths, the 464-square-meter suite has come to be known as a retreat for Hollywood celebrities. The scenes in the film Pretty Woman, by the way, were filmed on a studio set.

The original hotel, with its preserved 1910 facade facing Wilshire Boulevard. The E-shaped building is a combination of Italian Neo-Classic and Renaissance style. In back is the Beverly Wing.

The entrance to the Beverly Wing, a popular site for press conferences by movie stars. On the second floor is a passageway to the Wilshire Wing.

Right page: **Opening the door to The Penthouse Suite leads to a large hallway with Corinthian columns, which leads to a sitting area.**

The drawing room of The Penthouse Suite, which was built during the 1989 renovation of the hotel. The Federal-style design of the furnishings—the fireplace and paintings, mirror frame, wall lights, butterfly table and white plaster walls—is reminiscent of a Civil War-era mansion. The hotel's Presidential Suite is also on this floor.

The library is lined in white bookcases. In the center the master bedroom is visible.

Behind the bed in the master bedroom is a large wardrobe room. The central door leads to the library.

The second bedroom has a mirror-lined wardrobe.
The drapes above the bed are reproductions of a "half tester" design.

This bathroom has the most standard design of the suite's four bathrooms.
The oval mirror is particularly Hollywood in style. There is also a shower stall.

Colonnade Estate House

The Greenbrier
300 West Main St, White Sulphur Springs, West Virginia 24986 USA
Tel: (1-304) 536-1110 Fax: (1-304) 536-7834
http://www.greenbrier.com

Construction date: 1858 (the spa dates from around 1800)
Reconstruction date: 1911 (Bath Wing)
Architect: Firm of Harris & Richard
Interior design: Carleton Varney, Dorothy Draper & Company
Food & beverage facilities: 6
Guest rooms: 639 (including 46 suites), 69 cottages
Contact the hotel directly.

This historic resort is very American in feel. It started as a hot springs resort in 1780 with the construction of the first guest house. In 1858 the 228-room Grand Central Hotel opened. It was originally nicknamed "The White" because its chalk-white form stood out prominently in its all-green surroundings. When the Army of the South seemed headed for defeat the building was used as a hospital, and after the war General Robert E. Lee's summer home was used as a cottage. During the course of its history some 25 American presidents have stayed here.

The Colonnade Estate House was a three-story cottage built in 1838 at the Spring Row hot springs. In the basement are employees' quarters and storage space, with living spaces on the first floor and bedrooms on the second and third floors. One especially notable feature is the 24-person table in the dining room/meeting room, which has been used for secret meetings of presidents and dignitaries.

The main building of the present-day hotel, The Greenbrier, constructed next to the original hotspring town. The north side of the main hotel building is the original hotel, "The White."

The site plan of The Greenbrier. The old "Spring Row" hot springs are in the right-hand area of the hotel's main building. The summer house marks the source of the hot springs.
(Courtesy of The Greenbrier.)

The three-story porch of the Colonnade Estate House is visible above and to the left of the sightseeing coach. The neighborhood is filled with cottages convenient to the hot springs.
Right page: **The music room has a staircase done in Federal style, which was popular around 1780–1850. The room's fireplace and Ionic columns are also done in this style.**

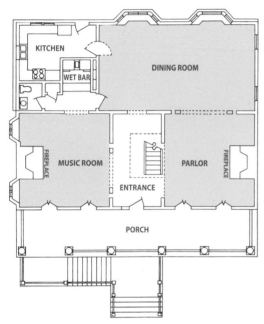

Floor plan of the ground floor of the Colonnade Estate House.
(Courtesy of The Greenbrier.)

The first-floor parlor. Although the word usuallly refers to a sitting area, in this case it serves as the entryway to the dining room. The two Ionic columns between the entrance and the music room (which features a grand piano) date back to pre-Civil War days. During the 1960s or 70s the interior fabrics used in the main building and cottages were coordinated by the interior designers, Carleton Varney, Dorothy Draper & Company. Here in the Colonnade Estate House the designers tried to recreate the original atmosphere of the building. An Empire-style chandelier hangs from the ceiling, and the armchairs are reproductions of 1730–1750 era Queen Anne-style pieces. The tips of the banisters have an unusual semi-circular shape. The table lamps were oringally Queen Anne candle stands. The mirror on the wall is a Federal-style antique dating from the 1790s.

The 24-person table in the dining/meeting room. Martin Van Buren, the eighth American president (served 1837–1841) dined at this table, and the servingware used here is the same as that used in the White House dining room.

The music room stairway.

The Ionic columns on the second-floor porch give it a Federal-style flavor.

An illustration of the cottage used by General Robert E. Lee after the Civil War. To the upper left is the Colonnade Estate House.

A basket with a rhododendron design (the floral symbol of the hotel) in the bathroom holds towels marked with the hotel logo. *Right page*: The second bedroom (Room 6217) with a queen-size bed. A warm blanket sits on top of the bed covers.

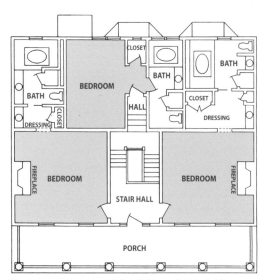

The second-floor plan of the Colonnade Estate House, which has three bedrooms, each with an attached bath.
(Courtesy of The Greenbrier.)

The main bedroom (Room 6216) includes a four-poster bed. The fabric of the bed covers, pillows, canopy, sofa and footrest all incorporate the rhododendron, the hotel's symbol, in their design. In the 18th century woods of briers, with pink flowers, surrounded the hot springs area.

Presidential Suite

The Hay Adams
800 16th Street NW., Washington, DC 20006 USA
Tel: (1-202) 638-6600   Fax: (1-202) 638-2716
http://www.lhw.com/hayadams

Opening date: Late spring,1928
Architect and Interior design:
  Mirhan Mesrobian/Wardman Company
Food & beverage facilities: 2
Guest rooms: 125, 20 suites
Contact: The Leading Hotels of the World

The hotel is named after John Hay, Secretary of State under President Theodore Roosevelt, and historian Henry Adams; the hotel was originally their mansion. The top-class Presidential Suite contains a drawing room, bedroom and bath. The drawing room is divided into a sitting area and a dining area, a simple and convenient arrangement, and the suite doesn't include a separate library or fancy separate dining room. The hotel sits in the midst of a neighborhood filled with government offices, and guests include business executives and government officials from all over the country. This is one of the buildings closest to the White House, and the suites are popular with guests who are visiting the White House.

Room service breakfast served in the drawing room of the Presidential Suite.

The facade of the hotel, with carriage porch.
To the left are Lafayette Park and the White House.

The magnificent nighttime view from the window includes
the White House and Reagan National Airport.
For White House security reasons permission is needed to
open the windows.

A footstool is used to
access the high bed.
Right: The bedroom
features unusual ceiling
rose ornaments and a
four-poster bed with
matching sofa.

Flower-petal plasterwork
decorates the ceiling of
the drawing room.

An Art Nouveau style desk in
the library of the Presidential Suite.
Right page: **The combination dining/meeting
room. There is a drawing room in
the corner of the library.**

Presidential Suite

The Peninsula, New York
700 Fifth Avenue, New York, NY 10019-4100 USA
Tel: (1-212) 956-2888   Fax: (1-212) 903-3943
http://www.peninsulahotels.com

Opening date: 1905
Architect: Hiss & Weeks
Food & beverage facilities: 3
Guest rooms: 185 rooms, 54 suites
Contact: The Peninsula Hotels

The original name was the Gotham Hotel, with 400 guest
rooms on 19 floors. The hotel started as an apartment
hotel, with butler service included. Ownership changed in
1988, and the hotel was renamed as Hotel Maxim's de
Paris. The interior was remodeled in Art Nouveau style, and
many furnishings from that period are still in use. In 1989
the hotel was purchased by The Hongkong and Shanghai
Hotels, Limited, and it became "The Peninsula, New York."
In 1998 all the rooms, including the Presidential Suite,
were renovated.

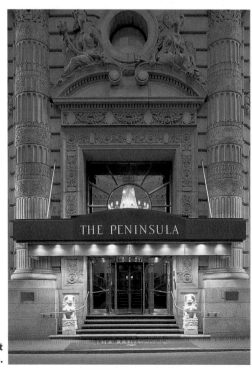

**A pair of lions stand at
the entrance.**

The bathroom has a large bathtub with jacuzzi.

A view of Fifth Avenue from the Presidential Suite.

Hanging from the wall are a photo and signed letter from French actress Sarah Bernhardt.
Right: The canopy bed in the main bedroom, decorated with beautiful fabric.

Penthouse Suite

The Plaza
Two Central Park South, New York, NY 10019 USA
Tel: (1-212) 546-5499   Fax: (1-212) 546-5324
http://www.fairmonthotels.com

Opening date: 1907
Architect: Henry J. Hardenbergh
Food & beverage facilities: 4
Guest rooms: 745, 60 suites
Contact the hotel directly

The Plaza Hotel, the giant castle on Central Park South, is not only a Manhattan landmark but it has also been designated as a National Historic Landmark. An earlier building was torn down and plans for the new hotel building were drawn up, with construction work handled by the firm of George A. Fuller Company. The owners were Harry S. Black (president of Fuller Construction and son-in-law of the founder), industrialist and well-known gambler John W. Gates, and investor Bernhard Beinecke. Construction work cost $12.5 million, a huge sum at the time. The design was by the famous architect Henry Janeway Hardenbergh, who fashioned the hotel after a German castle.

In 1970 the Penthouse Suite was built on the hotel's roof; it includes a private lobby opening onto a long corridor leading to three bedrooms, a drawing room and dining room. The decorative plasterwork on the ceilings of the rooms in the suite is especially notable, and it adds a warm touch to the interiors. Thanks in part to its excellent view of Central Park, this has come to be known as a "Super Suite" for VIP guests, and it costs upwards of $1600 per night.

A view of the hotel from a park with a statue of General Sherman. The Penthouse Suite is on the roof.

The ceiling rose (a round ceiling ornament that a chandelier hangs from), the wall moldings, the round decorative medallions above the doors, and the ceiling decorative moldings in the Penthouse Suite drawing room are a mix of Empire style and Louis XV style. The left-hand door leads to the dining room.

The gilt-frame mirror in the drawing room is a reproduction of a Chippendale design.

Right: **Marble statues of children stand on either side of the windows in the Penthouse Suite dining/meeting room, which is decorated in the same style as the drawing room. The beautiful red walls in the drawing room and the copper-colored walls in the dining room are decorated with silk fabric.**

The dining/meeting room, seen from the drawing room. The gilt medallion above the door is done in a "horn and ribbon" design.

The private lobby features a glass-dome ceiling and walls lined with bookcases. The hall to the left leads to the suite's three bedrooms.

Fairytale-themed wallpaper lines the walls of the hallway leading to the Penthouse Suite. *Right*: A bedroom with a canopy bed.

The canopy-bed-equipped bedroom has an attached bathroom; the sinks have swan-shaped faucets.

Cupid-design faucets can be found in the bathroom of another bedroom, which is furnished with a Corona bed.

A bedroom with a Corona bed. The armchair and footstool are Louis XV style. One of the best things about this suite is the sweeping panoramic view of Central Park.

Presidential Suite

Mandarin Oriental Hotel Majapahit, Surabaya
65 Jaran Tunjungan, Surabaya 60275, Indonesia
Tel: (62-31) 545-4333   Fax: (62-31) 545-9003
http://www.mandarinoriental.com

Opening date: 1910
Architect: J. Afprey
Renovation date: 1996
Interior design: Bent Severin & Associates International
Food & beverage facilities: 5
Guest rooms: 110, 40 suites
Contact: Mandarin Oriental Hotel Group

This hotel on Tunjungan Street in Surabaya, Indonesia's second-largest city, opened in 1910 as the Oranje Hotel. It was built by Lucas Martin Sarkies, a member of the family which established the Raffles Hotel in Singapore and the Strand Hotel in Yangon (Rangoon), Myanmar. In 1938 a new Art Deco-style public area was added to at the hotel entrance. During World War II the hotel was requisitioned by the Japanese army, and it was renamed the *Yamato Hoteru*.

In January 1966 the Mandarin Oriental Hotel Group reopened the hotel after a two-year, 3.2 billion-yen renovation project. At that time the 700-square-foot Presidential Suite was constructed on the hotel's first and second floors. There are four bedrooms on the second floor, and a drawing room, dining room, library and kitchen on the first floor. The interior is decorated in Indonesian style, with old musical instruments and the like; this is known as the most luxurious hotel suite south of Singapore.

Stained glass decorates the Art Deco-style entrance area.

The suite's private lobby, seen from a stair landing which features a stained-glass skylight.
Right page: The private lobby of the Presidential Suite. The inlay design in the floor is late-period English Georgian in style, a design used in Newby Hall in Yorkshire.

The person holding a child to the right of the photo is hotel king Lucas Martin Sarkies.
(Courtesy of Mandarin Oriental Hotel Majapahi, Surabaya.)

The drawing room has two separate sitting areas. Behind the stained glass partition in front is a card room, and at the back is the dining room. The large blue sofa was made in Indonesia and was based on the Scroll End Settee style of furniture that was popular in England in the 19th century.

The drawing room is sandwiched between the dining room on one side and a combination library and game room on the other.

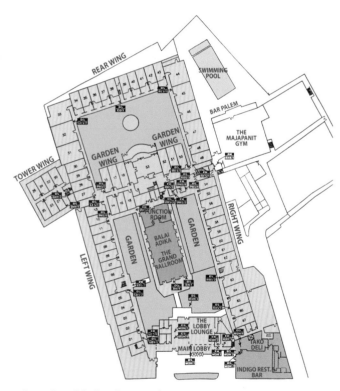

A floor plan of the hotel's ground floor. The original 1910 hotel had an A-shaped plan, with a courtyard in the center, and in 1938 the entrance area (visible in the lower part of the plan) was added. The Presidential Suite (Room 53) is in the central, red-colored area; when requested, rooms 14–19 can be connected to the second-floor master bedroom.

(Courtesy of Mandarin Oriental Hotel Majapahit Surabaya.)

The combination dining room and meeting room is provided with a large 16-person table; a seating area is to the left, and a 200-year-old hand-carved Arabic Door.

The drawing room can be separated from the master bedroom with a curtain rather than a door.
Right: The master bedroom is decorated in luxurious fabrics. To the left is the drawing room; there is also a separate wardrobe area. The sofa in back is a piece of furniture known as a "rest bed."

The master bedroom has its own drawing room, which can also serve as a library.

The enormous bathroom in the Presidential Suite features a large stool and a jacuzzi bath, and the interior is luxuriously appointed, suitable to its use by VIP guests. The large sinks with attached wood-framed mirrors were made in Indonesia.

Presidential Suite

InterContinental Resort Bali
Julan Uluwatsu 45, Jimbaran 80361, Bali, Indonesia
Tel: (62) 361-701-888   Fax: (62) 361-701-777
URL: http//www.ichotelsgroup.com

Opening date: March 8, 1993
Architect: Hendra Hadiprana
Interior design: Hendra Hadiprana
Guest rooms: 431, 18 suites, 2 villas
Contact: InterContinental Hotels Group

This large resort hotel is located on Jimbaran Bay in the southern part of Bali Island. The two-story Presidential Suite is set up for maximum privacy, and it has its own private pool and a unique Balinese-flavored interior. Architecture and interior design were handled by the Indonesian architect Hendra Hadiprana. He created a Western-style Presidential Suite, with private lobby, drawing room, dining room and kitchen on the first floor, but he also commissioned Balinese crafts, furnishings and paintings to create a Balinese-style atmosphere. In Bali there are villages inhabited by numerous local artists and craftsmen, and it was this cultural environment that he wanted to reflect with this interior.

There is also another Presidential Suite, decorated in a blue color scheme.

A private driveway leads to the private entrance.

The drawing room is decorated in a red color scheme. A dragon motif is used in the design of the sofa, and various Indonesian gods adorn the table lamp; the decor is heavy with Balinese character. To the rear is the dining room.

The two-story Bali InterContinental Resort sits in the middle of a wooded area,
and it was designed to blend in with the natural scenery of Jimbaran Bay Beach.

The combination dining room and meeting room, with gilt flower-petal designs adorning the ceiling and statues of Balinese gods in a corner of the room.
Right page: The warm, wood-grained private lobby has a center table decorated with gilt dragons. In back is the drawing room.

A private pool is included with the suite.

The design of the headboard in the master bedroom incorporates images of Balinese gods. The chair used with the dressing table and bed is a reproduction of a classic European piece called a "corridor stool" or a "window seat." *Right*: The sitting area of the master bedroom, on the second floor. There is a desk in the back of the room, and on the left is a reproduction of a classic English-style breakfront bookcase. To the left is the bed area.

The white-paneled walls of the second bedroom leave a fresh, clean impression.

The mirror-glass facade of the hotel, with large driveway.
Right page: **The drawing room of the Presidential Stateroom, seen from the dining room. In the very back is the bedroom.**

Presidential Stateroom

Hotel Istana Kuala Lumpur
73, Jalan Raja Chulan, 50200 Kuala Lumpur, Malaysia
Tel: (60-3) 241-9988 Fax: (60-3) 241-0111
http://www.meritus-hotels.com.sg

Opening date: 1992
Architect: Chao Tse Ann
Food & beverage facilities: 6
Guest rooms: 516 (including 64 suites)
Contact: Meritus Hotels & Resorts

This contemporary hotel is situated on one of the major thoroughfares in the Malaysian capital of Kuala Lumpur, Jalan Sultan Ismail. The building is on a four-acre site, and it stands 23 stories above ground and four below; total construction cost was 12 billion yen. The concept was to create a palace hotel for an Islamic country in a modern era; the word "Istana" means "palace" in Malaysian. The hotel is set up with world-class facilities and level of service, and the 64 suites and lounge on the 19th through 22nd floors are Mahkota Club floors with an extra-special level of service. The top-floor, contemporary-design Presidential Stateroom includes a private lobby, a combination dining room and meeting room, a drawing room with guest toilet and kitchen, a bedroom and a bathroom. The desk is furnished with a copy of the Koran, and a small green arrow on the ceiling points to Mecca.

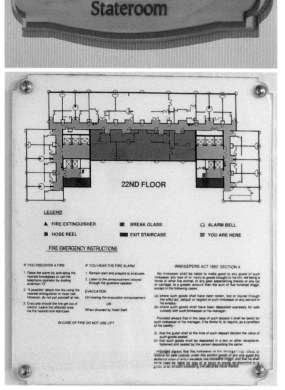

The door plate of the Presidential Stateroom.

A floor plan of the Presidential Stateroom.

The bathroom of the Presidential
Stateroom includes a bathtub
with jacuzzi.

The unique short four-poster bed in
the bedroom of the Presidential Stateroom.
Behind the window is the bathroom.

Presidential Suite

InterContinental Singapore
80 Middle Road, Bugis Junction, Singapore 188966
Tel: (65) 6338-7600 Fax: (65) 6338-7366
http://www.ichotelsgroup.com

Opening date: July 19, 1995
Architect: DP Architect
Interior design: Riffanbirg Associates
Food & beverage facilities: 8
Guest rooms: 406 (including 53 suites)
Contact: InterContinental Hotels Group

This new hotel was built in a redeveloped area of "shop houses"—with stores on the ground-floor level and residences above—that dates back to colonial days. Seventy shop houses were renovated and converted to guest rooms, and a 16-story tower was added to form the hotel. Part of the shop house street was turned into a covered, air-conditioned arcade, and department stores were added to attract visitors. The hotel offers a classic-style lobby-lounge where afternoon tea is served.

The interior of the top-floor Presidential Suite, with its thick columns, has a colonial-era feeling to it; even the color scheme is old-fashioned. The luxuriously spacious suite includes a private lobby, drawing room, dining room and kitchen, bedroom and bathroom.

The private lobby. In the back is the combination dining room and meeting room.
Right page: **The interior design of the drawing room of the Presidential Suite is a mix of Asian and Western influences.**

The door display for the Presidential Suite.

The hotel facade.
The redevelopment project included shop houses.

**The combination dining room
and meeting room is furnished
with a 12-person table, and an
unusual Chinese screen
decorates the wall.**

The bedroom, with four-poster bed.
Inside the cabinet under the flower
basket is a television set, and the room
also has a daybed.

Bath amenities include a take-home bag.

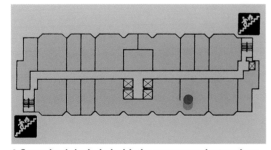

A floor plan is included with the emergency instructions on the back of the room's door. The Presidential Suite takes up the space of four ordinary guest rooms.

The bathroom, with oak walls and black granite floors.

The drawing room of the Amarin Suite,
with its eye-catching ceiling. There's also a
library, furnished with a desk in one corner.
Right page: The drawing room, seen from
the desk in the library. The room behind
the piano is the combination dining room
and meeting room

Amarin Suite

Grand Hyatt Erawan Bankok
494 Rajdamri Road, Bankok 10330, Thailand
Tel: (66-2) 254-1234 Fax: (66-2) 254-6308
http://www.hyatt.com

Opening date: December 1991
Architect: B & L Architects
Interior design: Oscar Llinas of Bilkey & Llinas Design
Food & beverage facilities: 5
Guest rooms: 380, 30 suites
Contact: Hyatt Hotels & Resorts

The Erawan Hotel was built on the grounds of
the original Erawan Temple. The Amarin Suite,
one of two top-class suites in the hotel, has a
wooden ceiling with an unusual design. The
furniture, bedcovers and so on use beautiful
Thai silk to help create an opulent air. The
suite is named after one of the hotel's owners,
the Amarin Company.

The 17-story guest-
room tower rises from
a four-story base.

The bathroom includes a powder-room area.

There is also a wooden ceiling in the suite's bedroom. The design of the bed, with claw-foot legs, is based on a piece of Royal Thai furniture

The Chairman's Suite

The Portman Ritz-Carlton, Shanghai
Shanghai Centre, 1376 Nanjing Xi Lu, Shanghai 200040, China
Tel: (86-21) 6279-8888   Fax: (86-21) 6279-8800
http://www.ritzcarlton.com

Opening date: January 1, 1990
Architect: John Portman
Interior design: Bilkey Llinas Design
Renovation dates: 1998, 2005
Food & beverage facilities: 7
Guest rooms: 578 (including 68 suites)
Contact: Tha Ritz Carton Hotel Company, L.L.C.

This 50-story castle of commerce sits on Shanghai's busy entertainment and shopping street Nanjing Xi Lu. The owners are a syndicate of investors from China, America, Hong Kong and Japan, led by hotel developer and architect John Portman. The Chairman's Suite is one of five top-class suites on the hotel's top floor. It includes a bedroom, drawing room, and combination dining room and meeting room. The drawing room and dining room walls are decorated with reproductions of 1840s-era photos of Shanghai and paintings of Shanghai and Hong Kong harbors.

The hotel facade,
with residential wings on either suide.

The drawing room is furnished with a large desk. The liquid-crystal display television rotates 360 degrees, so that it can also be used in the dining room.

The combination dining/meeting room in the Chairman's Suite.
On the left-hand wall hangs a reproduction of a 1840s painting of Shanghai's Bund.

A double bed in the bedroom of the Chairman's Suite.

A bedroom with twin beds. (Located in the front portion of the left page.)

Royal Suite

Okura Garden Hotel Shanghai
58 Mao Ming Road(S), Shanghai 200020, China
Tel: (86-21) 6415-1111 Fax: (86-21) 6415-8866
http://www.lhw.com/okurashang

Construction date: 1926 (French Club)
Opening date: March 10, 1990
Architect: Obayashi Corporation
Interior design: Kanko Kikaku Sekkeisha
Food & beverage facilities: 7
Guest rooms: 445 rooms, 47 suites
Contact: The Leading Hotels of the World

Originally built as the French Club in the old French settlement area of Shanghai, the hotel had a tower added when it started life as a hotel in 1990. When the hotel first opened it was managed by Japan's Okura Hotel company. It went through its first renovation in 1999-2003, and a second phase is scheduled for 2004-2008, for a total cost of 1.7 billion yen. In 2005 the Continental Room French restaurant and the Sky Bar on the top floor of the tower were remodeled, and the Sazanka teppanyaki restaurant was opened.

The Royal Suite is one of the hotel's top-class suites, and renovation work on it was completed in 2004. Rather than creating an ultra-modern interior, the decorative goal of the renovation was to create a fusion of Chinese, Japanese and Western cultures suitable to the "Okura Garden Hotel." This is one of the remodeled rooms and suites on the hotel's 26th-28th floors, which are Executive Floors with a premium level of service. Construction work, during which shower stalls were added to the bathrooms, was completed in April 2005.

Inside the large space of the study is a combination dining/meeting space and a desk area.
Right page: **The drawing room of the Royal Suite includes two separate sitting areas and a guest toilet.**

The hotel's facade; behind the original building which was the French Club during the era of the French Settlement a new 34-story guest-room tower was built.

The bathroom of the Royal Suite.
In the left corner is a sauna room,
and in back is a toilet.

The bedroom of the Royal Suite.

Presidential Suite

Gold Coast Hotel
No.1 Castle Peak Roard, Castle Peak Bay
Kowloon, Hong Kong, China
Tel: (852) 2452-8833 Fax: (852) 2440-7368
http://www.goldcoasthotel.com.hk/

Opening date: August 28, 1993
Architect: Wong & Ouyang (HK) Ltd.
Interior design: Leese Robertson Freeman Designers Limited
Construction company: Tat Lee Construction Co., Ltd.
Food & beverage facilities: 5
Guest rooms: 450 (including 57 suites)
Contact the hotel directly.

This is "Hong Kong's first resort hotel," opened in a beachfront development area 30 kilometers west of central Hong Kong. The 110-acre grounds of this huge project include five top-class residential towers, 14 towers with luxury lease apartments, a 300-boat marina and this hotel. The developer was the Sino Group, a hotel and real estate development company. The total cost of the project was HK$2.64 billion, of which the hotel cost HK$600 Million.

The well-situated Presidential Suite is a duplex on the 10th and 11th floors of the hotel; the upper floor has a bedroom and bathroom, and below that is a drawing room with an impressive curving staircase.

The hotel, seen from the tennis courts. All rooms have ocean views.

The drawing room includes a seating area, a desk and a stairway. The bedroom is above. The right-hand door leads to the dining room.

The combination dining/meeting room.
In the rear is a small kitchen.

Room service breakfast served in
the seating area of the drawing room

The bathroom includes a bathtub with jacuzzi.

There is a concave mirror on the headboard of
the bed in the master bedroom.

Churchill's former breakfast room has been redecorated and has become the Salon Winston Churchill, available for parties and events.

English King Edward VIII, who abdicated the throne to marry Mrs. Simpson, at a hotel party. The Greenbrier, White Sulpher Springs, West Virginia, USA
(Courtesy of The Greenbrier.)

A PR poster for the Monaco Grand Prix, an early pioneer in the Formula One racing world.

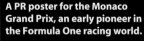

MONACO
8 AOUT 1937

Opposite page: **Yellow cloth covers the walls and ceiling of the drawing room in the Appartement Winston Churchill. The interior was redone in 1998. Hotel de Paris, Monte Carlo, Monaco**

World-famous celebrities have their favorite hotels, and often hotels that have been favored by famous people will create special rooms commemorating their visits. In this chapter we'll introduce nine celebrity suites named after various kings, princes, statesmen, singers, writers, architects, and designers.

Among the countless famous guests of the pioneering Hotel de Paris resort hotel—Russian Grand-duc Vladimir, the English Crown Prince (later Edward VIII), Belgian King Leopold II, 20th-century financiers Baron Henri de Rothschild and Pierpont Morgan and so on—the hotel chose to name its top-class suite after Winston Churchill. During his later years, in the 1950s and 1960s, Churchill would come here to stay every winter. To protect his privacy, the room next to his suite was used as his breakfast room, and a private passageway was created. Years later, the hotel created the top-class Appartement Winston Churchill in his honor.

Fashion queen Coco Chanel is another celebrity, although not everyone is aware that that this glittering star of the Paris scene spent her last days at the Hotel Ritz, where she died. Fifteen years after retiring, at the age of 71, she returned to the fashion world and introduced a new style of tailored suit. Although critical reaction was harshly negative, the suits were an instant hit with American businesswomen, and the "Chanel Suit" was reborn. It is perhaps a fittingly stylish story that the queen of fashion revived her career and lived out the remainder of her life here, the top-class Parisian hotel founded by hotel king Cesar Ritz. A half-century later the small Suite Coco Chanel is a treasured jewel within the hotel. Chanel is an international brand, now run by designer Karl Lagerfeld, and when the international fashion community gathers for the Paris collection, reservations in the Chanel Suite are highly coveted.

La Suite Churchill

La Mamounia
Avenue Bab Jdid, Marrakech, Morocco
Tel: (212-44) 38-86-00 Fax: (212-44) 44-49-40
http://www.ihw.com/lamamounia

Opening date: 1923
Architect: A. Marchisio & Henri Prost
Additional construction dates: 1953, 1977
Renovation date: 1986
Guest rooms: 171, 57 suites, 3 villas
Contact: The Leading Hotels of the World

La Suite Churchill is the suite where Mr. and Mrs. Churchill came every winter to escape the cold during their later years. The suite was originally on a different floor, but it was moved when construction work was done on the hotel; it has wooden walls and English Regency-style furniture.

When outdoors or in the suite's anteroom Churchill used to enjoy whiskey from a portable flask, and he painted regularly. Although he was better known for his hobby of bricklaying he was also an avid painter. One of Churchill's hats and a favorite walking stick can be found in the drawing room, along with an unfinished painting by him of the Atlas Mountains and a lake.

A view of the pool from the balcony of La Suite Churchill. The building on the right is a villa. The snow-covered Atlas Mountains can be seen during the clear days of winter.

The drawing room of
La Suite Churchill
(Room 330).
The sofa is known as
a "club sofa" or a
"Chesterfield couch."

Portraits and photos hang in the drawing room of La Suite Churchill.
Right: **The master bedroom in La Suite Churchill. The "simple canopy" design, with drapes hanging from metal rods, was fashionable in France around 1836.**

A bronze statue of Churchill in the drawing room.

The guest room display is Art Deco in style.

Suite Coco Chanel

Ritz Paris
15 Place Vendome, 75001 Paris, France
Tel: (33-1) 43-16-30-30   Fax: (33-1) 43-16-36-68
http://www.lhw.com/ritzparis

Opening date: 1889
Architect: Charles Mewes
Renovation date: 1988
Food & beverage facilities: 4
Guest rooms: 106, 56 suites
Contact: The Leading Hotels of the World

The Suite Coco Chanel is one of the two rooms used by Chanel as office and residence; it is filled with the Chinese-style furniture favored by Chanel. The suite is located on the third floor (three flights above the ground floor), and offers an excellent view of Place Vendome from its bay window. It's said that everyone in the world of fashion wants to stay here once, and it is one of the attractions of the Ritz Paris. (In 2002 the long-established Hotel Ritz changed its name to the "Ritz Paris.")

The door display for the Suite Coco Chanel.

The hotel facade on Place Vendome.
The second-floor windows have bulletproof glass.

Because of its position behind the roof-top bay windows, the Suite Coco Chanel has slanted walls which give it an unusual shape. The Chinese-style screens were used by Chanel herself.

The sofa and twin night tables were among Chanel's favorites. Photos of Chanel in her later years hang from the walls.
Right: The view of Place Vendome and the Austerlitz Column that Chanel would have seen from the suite. Perhaps she celebrated here with champagne when her Chanel suits came back into fashion and became hugely popular in America.

A large-size Chinese-style ceramic table lamp used by Chanel.

The Chinese-style wardrobe was owned by Chanel.

Duke of York Suite

The Royal Crescent Hotel
16 Royal Crescent, Bath, BA1 2LS, England, UK
Tel: (44-1225) 823-333   Fax: (44-1225) 339-401
http://www.royalcrescent.com

Construction date: 1775
Architect: John Wood the Younger
Opening date: 1989
Food & beverage facilities: 3
Guest rooms: 47 (including 22 suites)
Contact the hotel directly.

This hotel was constructed from two residences, No. 15 and No. 16, at the center of the Royal Crescent in Bath. The building was originally constructed with luxurious residences for long-term use by wealthy visitors to the Bath spa resort area during Georgian times. The residence at No. 16 was used by the second son of King George III, the Duke of York, and it is after him that the hotel's top-class suite is named. When the hotel opened, the building's late Hanover dynasy interior was restored, and neo-classic-style furnishings were used to create an atmosphere evocative of that time period. The interiors in the 47 guest rooms are all done in different interior fabrics.

The door plate of the Duke of York Suite.

A view of the Royal Crescent building from near the hotel entrance.

The Duke of York Suite has a late Georgian-period flavor. The antique sofa, on eight casters, is a George III mahogany settee.

A portrait of the Duke hangs over the fireplace in the Duke of York Suite.

The ceiling of the Duke of York Suite is adorned with colored carved plasterwork with a design of swans and flower pots; these late Georgian-period works have been magnificently restored.

One of the fireplace ornaments.

The suite's bathroom, originally a baggage room.

The hotel entrance, at No. 16.

The Royal Crescent is a Georgian crescent structure on a hill looking out over the hot-springs resort town of Bath, which dates back to Roman times. The basic plan for the crescent was devised by architect John Wood, and the plan was carried out by his son, John Wood the Younger. Construction work took eight years, and the 170-meter crescent was completed in 1775. Since then it has come to be known as one of the masterpieces of 18th-century English urban architecture. The stucture also included stable facilities for coach horses. The crescent building was divided into thirty separate residences, and those were first used by aristocrats of the day who were visiting the spas at Bath. In 1768 French Queen Marie Antoinette also paid a visit.

The hotel's check-in area uses a single desk; this was originally an entrance hall. In back is the hotel cashier and a staircase.

Suite Colette

Le Richemond
Jardin Brunswick, 1201 Geneve, Switzerland
Tel: (41-22) 715-7000 Fax: (41-22) 715-7001
http://www.richemond.com

Opening date: 1875
Food & beverage facilities: 3
Guest rooms: 67, 31 suites
Contact the hotel directly

The Le Richemond started out as a pension run by Armleder family, and the hotel was managed by three generations of that family as it became a Geneva landmark. In 2003 it was purchased by the Rocco Forte Hotels company.

After the top-class Presidential Suite, next in line is the hotel's Suite Colette. It was named after the writer Sidonie Gabrielle Claudine Colette, a frequent guest of the hotel who was known for her "Claudine" series of novels among many other books.

The Suite Colette (Rooms 610-611-612-614) is elegantly appointed, with red-and-gray curtains at the windows and the same fabric around the suite's doorframes. Fabric drapes on the light tables also help create a warm atmosphere. All the hotel's bathrooms have heated floors, and the hotel, well situated on Lake Geneva, welcomes guests even during the snowy winter months.

The hotel facade. Connected on the right-hand side is another hotel, the same layout as when the hotel was first established as a pension.

The door plate for the Colette Suite has a feminine floral pattern. Below is the door knocker, with the hotel's name.
Right page: **The drawing room (Room 610-611) of the Colette Suite. The portrait is of Colette when she was young.**

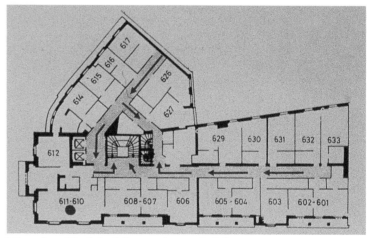

A floor plan of the Suite Colette on the top, sixth floor.
Upon request, rooms 606-607-608 can also be attached to the suite.
(Courtesy of Le Richemond.)

The drawing room (Rooms 610-611) of the Suite Colette. The front door connects to the adjacent suite (rooms 606-607-608), and the master bedroom (room 614) is also connected.

The wall design of the headboard side of the master bedroom (Room 612) of the Suite Colette. Classic drape-style curtains are used.

The master bedroom of the Suite Colette.
Beyond the center door is an additional bedroom, Room 614.

The bathroom in the Suite Colette. Done in marble and granite, the bathroom includes a shower stall and a heated floor system.

From the small balcony of the Suite Colette you can see Lake Geneva and Mont Blanc. Below is Brunswick Garden.

Between the drawing room and the master bedroom is a combination dining room and meeting room. The drawing room side of the door is decorated in unusual red and gray silk curtains. The dining room walls are covered in dramatic red and black wallpaper. At the right end of the dining room is a private lobby.

Doge Suite

Hotel Danieli
Castello 4196, Venezia 30122, Italy
Tel: (39-41) 522-6480   Fax: (39-41) 520-0208
http://www.starwoodhotels.com

Construction date: 14th century
Opening date: 1822
Renovation date: 1989, 2001
Food & beverage facilities: 3
Guest rooms: 227, 36 suites
Contact: Starwood Hotels & Resorts

This prestigious, historical hotel occupies one of the world's oldest buildings. It was originally built as a family mansion in the 14th century by descendents of Enrico Dandolo, Doge of the Republic of Venice in the early 13th century and one of the leaders of the Fourth Crusade. During those days Venetian aristocrats also took part in trade and government, and the original building reflected that—the first floor was used for offices and a commercial warehouse, and on the second floor were lodgings for foreign visitors; the family lodgings were on the third floor.

The Doge Suite in the present hotel was created for the use of well-to-do visitors from Europe and the Middle East, and the three adjoining suites can also be connected. The glittering red and blue of the Murano glass lamps hanging in the suite's rooms and galleries gives the suite a real feeling of Venetian opulence.

Over the course of its 600-year history the building has undergone extensive repair and renovation work. During the 1989 renovation the wooden ceilings and ceiling moldings were restored and regilded, and the interior was restored in such manner as to create the atmosphere of a lodging for honored guests in the mansion of the Doge.

To the right is the five-story Hotel Danieli. In the center is the Danielino wing, and in back is the new Casa Nuova wing. The building with the tower was originally the Palazzo Ducale, which boasted an ideal location in Venice.

The drawing room of the Doge Suite, with a large-size Venetian-style antique mirror dating back to around 1800. It was originally a reception hall that served Catholic cardinals and European nobility during the middle ages, and in later years the sons and daughters of the British aristocracy when they went on their "Grand Tour" of Europe.

Hanging from the walls of the drawing room are portraits of four members of the Dandolo family chosen by the Doge, and above the fireplace is a family crest with helmet and sword. The Venetian giltwood throne is a reproduction of an 18th-century piece.

Murano Glass is made on Murano Island, next to Venice, and the glass-making technique is well guarded. Seeing the flickering lights of hundreds of shining through red and blue glass of the chandeliers hanging inside the hotel, one can imagine the world where honored guests stayed here during medieval times.

The bedroom walls in the Doge Suite are lined with cushions and covered in silk fabric.

The wall light in the bedroom is also made from Murano Glass.

The walls of the bathroom in the Doge Suite are white marble. The bathroom includes a small shower stall.

A portrait of Enrico Dandolo, the Venetian Doge whose name lives on in the history books. During the time of the Crusades he was over 80 years old and nearly blind.
Right page:
The bedroom of the Doge Suite. The plaster ceiling is decorated with a fresco painting by 19th-century artist Iacopo Guarana of four cupids flying in the heavens.

Suite Tchaikovsky

Hotel Londra Palace
Riva Degli Schiavoni 4171, 30122 Venezia, Italy
Tel: (39-041) 520-0533   Fax: (39-041) 522-5032
http://www.slh.com/londra/

Opening data: *c.* 1835
Architect: Three Architects Ltd, Dallas
Renovation date: 2000
Interior design: Rocco Manori
Food & beverage facilities: 2
Guest rooms: 53, 20 suites
Contact: Small Luxury Hotels of the World

The hotel first opened in 1835 as a two-story wooden building called the Alberghi d'Inghilterra, which catered to wealthy English travelers of the day. In 1860 the present structure took form, and the name was changed to Londres e Beau Rivage. The young composer Tchaikovsky stayed here in 1870, when he was still in his thirties and employed as a teacher at the newly established Moscow Music University. He worked on his Fourth Symphony, one of his early masterpieces, during his stay. Photos of Tchaikovsky and musical scores now hang from the walls of the room where he stayed, Room 106. The walls, floor, curtains and so on are decorated with a typically Italian red color scheme. The gold print on the red wallpaper is a French "fleur de lis" design.

**The facade of
the five-story Hotel Londra Palace.**

Suite Tchaikovsky consists of a bedroom and bathroom. The lower portion of the Ionic columns have an unusual inlay design. Hanging above the writing desk is a photographic portrait of Tchaikovsky at the time of his stay in the hotel.

There's a view of San Giorgio Maggiore Island from the front of Suite Tchaikovsky, and to the left is Lido Island.
Right page: Decorating the wall of the drawing room is an unusual large gilt wood carving with a theme of music and musical instruments. Bedstools flank either side of the "sleigh" style bed.

Reproductions of letters and music scores by Tchaikovsky and photos of the Swan Lake and other ballet performances hang from the walls.

The doortag to request room cleaning shows a drawing of a woman cleaning, with text in Italian and English.

Frank Lloyd Wright Suite

The Plaza
Two Central Park South, New York, NY 10019 USA
Tel: (1-212) 546-5499 Fax: (1-212) 546-5324
http://www.fairmonthotels.com

Opening date: 1908
Architect: Henry Janeway Hardenberg
Interior design: James Nothcut Associates
Food & beverage facilities: 5
Guest rooms: 745, 60 suites
Contact the hotel directly.

The landmark Plaza Hotel, a castle built on Central Park South, is often said to embody the spirit of New York. Since its opening it has been famous as a favorite destination of everyone from guests of state and politicians to business tycoons and opera singers. One famous guest was architect Frank Lloyd Wright, who used the hotel as an office, design studio and bedroom while he was building the Guggenheim Museum. Wright died several months after completing the museum, and the three rooms he used were transformed into a suite bearing his name. With the permission of the Frank Lloyd Wright Foundation, the suite was furnished with reproductions of Wright-designed furniture and architectural drawings.

The side of the present hotel back entrance (Fifth Avenue entrance). The first through third floors are covered in marble, with granite covering floors 4–19 and a gable roof and tower on floors 14–19.

The drawing room of the Frank Lloyd Wright Suite, which was used as an office by Wright. Drawings by Wright hang on either side of the fireplace, and the screen panels on the walls are reproductions of Wright designs.

A simple easy chair designed by Wright.

The Frank Lloyd Wright Suite uses Rooms 221–223.

A reproduction of a candle table light designed by Wright.

The Plaza Hotel in 1906 when it was under construction.
(Courtesy of The Plaza.)

The suite's small second bedroom (Room 223),
which was the space used by Wright as a bedroom.

A portrait of Frank Lloyd Wright in
his later years hangs from the wall.

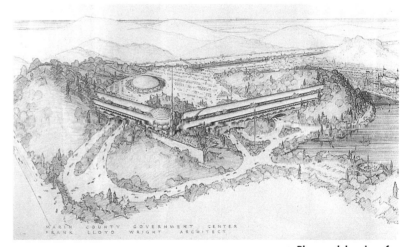

Plans and drawings for
the Guggenheim Museum and
private residences hang from
the walls in the master bedroom.

The Art Deco style bathroom.
Behind the glass door is a shower stall;
the bathtub is separate.

A reproduction of a stained glass window designed by Wright in 1912 for the Avery Coonley Playhouse hangs from a wall in the master bedroom.

The master bedroom of the Frank Lloyd Wright Suite. The Wright-designed table uses specially designed chairs. The white book rack on the table is also his design. Wright-designed pieces are used with the permission of the Frank Lloyd Wright Foundation. This bedroom as used as Wright's design office.

Jacqueline Kennedy Suite

Raffles Hotel Le Royal
92 Rukhak Vithei Daun Penh (off Monivong Boulevard)
Sangkat Wat Phnom, Phnom Penh, Kingdom of Cambodia
Tel: (855-23) 981-888   Fax: (855-23) 981-168
http://www.raffles.com

Opening date: 1929
Architect: Ernest Hebrard
Additional construction & renovation date: 1997
Renovation consultants: Architects 61
Interior design: Concept International Design Group
Food & beverage facilities: 7
Guest rooms: 169, 26 suites
Contact: Raffles International Hotels & Resorts

Hotel Le Royal first opened during French colonial days in 1929 as a 54-room hotel. The architect Ernest Hebrard designed five new hotels for the government of French Indochina, and also handled city planning for Phnom Penh. Jacqueline Kennedy, widow of President John F. Kennedy who was later married to wealthy businessman Aristotle Onassis, visited the city and stayed at the hotel in 1967, after Cambodia had gained independence. A guest room with a white four-poster bed was arranged for her stay. In 1997, after the end of the long civil war, the hotel was rebuilt, and it reopened with 210 guest rooms. These included the Jacqueline Kennedy Suite, which was furnished with the restored original bed that was used during her stay.

The back of the old hotel building. An outdoor pool and a new wing (on the left) were added later.

The Jacqueline Kennedy Suite is in the old wing of the hotel.

The claw-foot bathtub and simple sink in the bathroom help recreate the atmosphere of the time of Kennedy's visit. *Right*: A biography of Jacqueline Kennedy, the widow of President Kennedy, is on the desk of the suite.

A photo of King Sihanouk with Jacqueline Kennedy

Noel Coward Suite

The Oriental, Bangkok
48 Oriental Avenue, Bangkok 10500, Thailand
Tel: (66-2) 659-9000 Fax: (66-2) 659-9284
http://www.mandarinoriental.com

Opening date: May 15, 1887
Architect: S. Cardu
Renovation date: 2000
Dining facilities: 10
Guest rooms: 362, 34 suites
Contact: Mandarin Oriental Hotel Group

A wooden guesthouse called The Oriental occupied this site around 1860, but it was destroyed by fire. In 1870 it was rebuilt with the same name, and purchased by Hans Niels Andersen, a shipping industry tycoon. The 1887 two-story, 10-room stone building was repaired; this is the present-day "Authors' Residence." Former sailor turned author Joseph Conrad, Somerset Maugham, Ernest Hemingway and dozens of other writers have stayed here during their travels to Southeast Asia, and their visits have been commemorated with suites on the second floor of the old wing of the hotel. One such suite is named after Noel Coward, known as a playwright, film writer, author, composer and actor, who wrote one of his plays during his stay here.

A portrait of Noel Coward hangs in the bedroom of the suite. He was the scriptwriter for the David Lean-directed films. This Happy Breed (1944), Blithe Spirit (1945) and Brief Encounter (1945), and he won a special Academy Award in 1943. He also appeared as an actor in "Paris When It Sizzles" (1963) along with William Holden and Audrey Hepburn. *Right page*: The drawing room of the Noel Coward Suite, furnished with bamboo chairs and Thai paintings, has a Southeast-Asian feel to it. The semi-circular carving at the top of the door frame dates back to the original construction of the Authors' Residence.

A bird's-eye view of the hotel, which also has facilities on the opposite shore of the river.
(Courtesy of The Oriental Bangkok.)

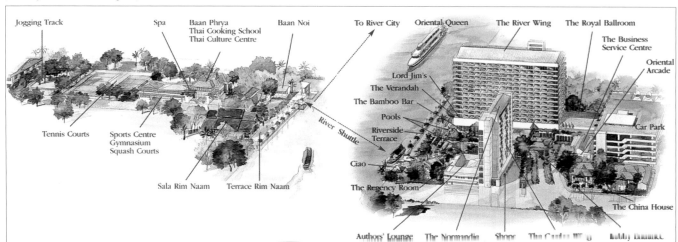

The powder room next to the bedroom has a unique shade light with a mirror frame.
Right: **The bathroom features a claw-foot bathtub with Victorian-style faucets and soap holder, and a triangular shower stall. There are also a toilet, bidet, and a single sink.**

A silk bathrobe used in the Noel Coward Suite.

Specially made hand-carved keyholders are used for the Noel Coward Suite and the other suites in the Authors' Residence.

The bedroom of the Noel Coward Suite, decorated in Royal Thai style with gilt four-poster twin beds. A door leads to the powder room.

Profile

Hiro Kishikawa

Photo-journalist

Hiro Kishikawa was born in 1951 in Otaru City on Hokkaido, Japan. After traveling about 50 countries of the world as a movie cameraman for FIS World Cup Ski Races and WRC (World Rally Championship), in 1982 he switched to a photo-journalist and specialized in photographing some 400 first-class hotels around the world as his life's work. He is a regular contributor to several magazines such as *Traveller* (Conde Nast), *The Gold* (JCB Card) and *Impression* (Amex).

Main works for the advertising media: Hino Motors' calendar in 1987 *Windows of the World* that won a prize in a Japanese nation-wide calendar competition, Renault's advertisement *1999 LUTECIA*, Fuji Film's brochure *1998, 2000, PHOTO-KINA*, and many others.

Main published works: *Great Hotels of the World* and *Classic Hotels of the World*— each 6 volume photograph collections with bilingual texts, published by Kawade Shobo Shinsha. These books can be bought at bookstores of many countries and at Web sites of Amazon.com, Barnes & Noble, Yahoo, and so on.

http://www.kplann.com (Hotel Maniac Era)
hiro@kplann.com
Contact: **KEI. PLANNING**

Noboru Kawazoe

Architectural Critic

Born in 1926 in Tokyo, Japan, Mr. Noboru Kawazoe graduated from Department of Architecture, Waseda University. After the chief editor (1953–57) of the magazine "Shinkenchiku" (New Architecture), he became an architectural critic and organized "Group Metabolism" with architects and designers in 1959. While serving as member of Japanese executive committee of World Design Conference (1960), sub-producer of Expo Osaka's theme-pavilions (1969), visiting professor of Waseda University (1993–96), he founded the think tank CDI in Kyoto in 1970 and Japan Society of Lifology in 1972. He is now the representative of CDI.

Mr. Kawazoe was received Mainichi Publication Culture Awards in 1960 by his book *Dwellings of Gods and the People*, Kon Wajiro Award in 1982 by *Proposal of the Lifology*, and Minakata Kumagusu Award in 1997.

Main published works: *What is Design?* (Kadokawa Shoten), *Dwellings of Gods and the People* (Kobunsha), *Proposal of the Lifology* (Domes Shuppan), *Kon Wajiro* (Chikuma Shobo), and many other books.